KU-687-132

SURVIVAL IN THE DESERTS

by Jane and David Glover

Illustrated by Brian Watson

Brimax Books · Newmarket · England

Acknowledgements
Frank Lane Picture Agency: 14 (A Christiensen); 17 (M Van Nostrand);
24 (B Langrish)
NHPA: 22U (R J Erwin); 26 (S Dalton); 33 (S Dalton)
Oxford Scientific Films: 10B (F Ehrenstrom); 13U (T Leach);
15U (S Osolinski); 16U (R Packwood); 16B (S Osolinski); 23 (R Cao Ba);
27U (Z Leszczynski); 27B (Z Leszczynski); 28U (R Jackman);
28B (A Ramage); 36 (K Atkinson); 37B (R Kuiter)
Picturepoint London: 10U; 18B; 37M
Survival Anglia: 13B (M Linley); 15B (J and D Bartlett); 18U (M Linley);
15B (J and D Bartlett); 18U (M Linley); 19 (J Foott)

Deserts

Hot deserts are very uncomfortable places for animals to live. There is hardly any water to drink and very few plants can grow. During the day the rocks and sand get too hot to touch and at night it is freezing cold. But many different animals still manage to live in these harsh conditions.

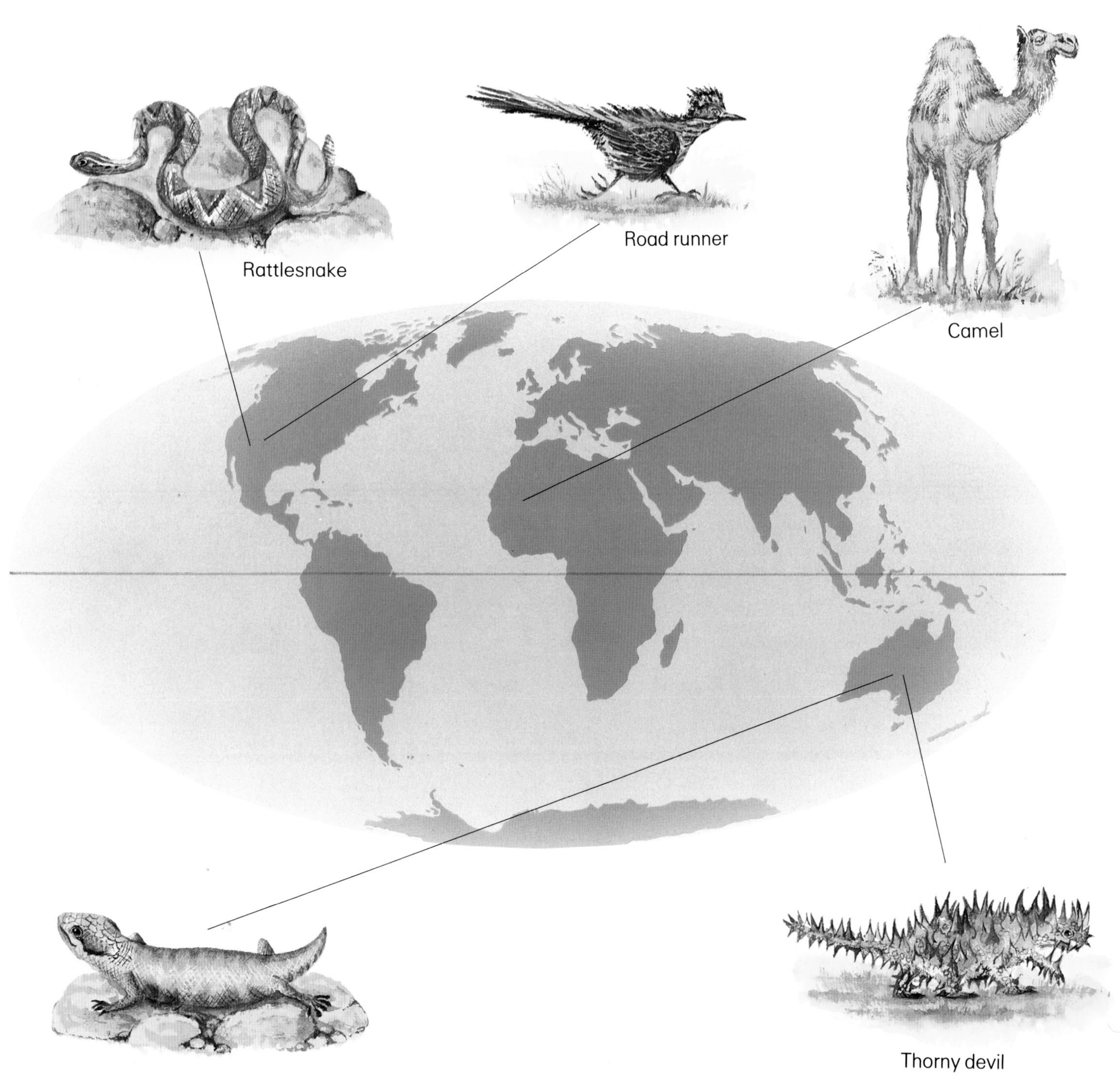

Africa and Arabia

The Sahara Desert in Africa is the biggest desert in the world. Some parts are very sandy. The wind piles the sand into huge dunes that stretch for hundreds of miles. Other parts are flat and rocky. In some places there are mountains.

In the middle of the desert it may not rain for years on end. Very few plants and animals can survive in this harsh place. Most animals live on the edge of the desert or around oases where there is water and plants can grow.

At oases, camels feed on the plants and drink gallons of water at a time. They can travel for days from one oasis to another without eating or drinking.

Antelopes and gazelles wander for miles browsing on dry grass and the few bushes which they find.

Smaller animals like jerboas, gerbils and birds feed on seeds which they look for in the sand.

The plant and seed eaters are hunted by predators like the cheetah, fennec fox and lanner falcon.

The poisonous scorpion hunts insects and spiders. Sometimes it will catch a small lizard or a mouse.

The dromedary

The dromedary is a camel with one hump. There are no wild dromedaries left in the desert. All the camels in Africa and Arabia are kept by local people who ride them and use them to carry loads.

The dromedary's hump is not full of water. It is full of fat. As the camel travels across the desert it uses the fat for energy instead of eating food. The camel manages to go without water for so long because it hardly sweats. Its shaggy fur traps a layer of cool air against its body. Even if the camel gets really hot it still feels comfortable and can cool down at night.

There are often sandstorms in the desert and the camel has cleverly adapted to these conditions. It has long eyelashes to keep the sand out of its eyes and special muscles to close its nostrils. Its big feet stop it sinking into the soft sand, as the sand is blown about.

Antelopes and gazelles

The addax and the oryx are desert antelopes. They are now very rare. You can tell them apart by their horns; the addax's are curly, the oryx's are straight.

The addax live in Africa. They gather in small herds and wander over the desert looking for grass. They never drink from a stream or a pool. They get all the water they need from the grass and the dew that settles on it in the mornings.

Oryx used to be common in Arabia but man has nearly hunted them to extinction.

From the side, the oryx looks as though it has just one long, straight horn. Some people think that this is how the legend of the unicorn, a white horse with a single horn, may have started.

Dorcas gazelles are tiny antelopes. If one of the herd spots danger, perhaps a cheetah, it warns the others by raising its tail to show the white patch on its rump, then the whole herd runs off.

Jerboas and sand grouse

Jerboas are small rodents like mice and hamsters. During the day it is too hot for small animals on the desert sand so they stay underground in their burrows. Jerboas are nocturnal. This means that they come out at night to feed. They gnaw seeds, shoots and grass with their sharp teeth.

There are very few plants in the desert so jerboas must travel long distances to find enough to eat. They move quickly, hopping like kangaroos on their strong back legs. Their long tails help them to balance.

Sand grouse eat only dry seeds so they must find water to drink. Every day they fly many miles to the nearest pool or lake.

The sand grouse's nest is a simple hollow in the sand. The female lays two or three eggs and takes it in turn with the male to sit on them. When the chicks hatch the male brings them water. As he drinks his breast feathers get wet and the chicks suck those for water when he gets back to the nest.

Desert hunters

The cheetah is the fastest land animal in the world. It can run at speeds of up to 70 mph (112kph) to catch gazelles and young antelopes. When it gets close enough it trips up its prey with its paws and kills it with a bite to the throat.

Some people who live in the desert train cheetahs to hunt for them. They call them hunting leopards. Wild cheetahs are now extinct in Arabia and have become rare in the Sahara, but they are more common in the grasslands to the south.

The fennec fox is well adapted to life in the desert. It has big ears to help it to lose heat and stay cool. During the day it stays in a deep burrow where it rests in the cool. It hunts at night, using its huge ears to listen for jerboas, insects and other small animals. Like many desert animals the fennec does not drink. It gets all the water it needs from its food.

Lanner falcons soar high above the desert. They can spot the movement of a jerboa or a lizard a thousand feet below. Sometimes a pair of lanners hunt together. The female skims along the ground to frighten a small bird into the air. When it flies up the male dives down to catch it from above.

Locusts and scorpions

It does rain sometimes in the desert and when it does the dry seeds that have been lying under the sand sprout and grow quickly. Insects that have been waiting for the right conditions hatch and feed on this new plant growth. Locusts breed rapidly and if there is enough plant growth there may soon be millions of them. When the locusts have eaten all the plants in one place, they take off in a swarm to search for new food. Some swarms are so big they make the sky seem black. A large swarm can destroy farmers' crops in a few hours.

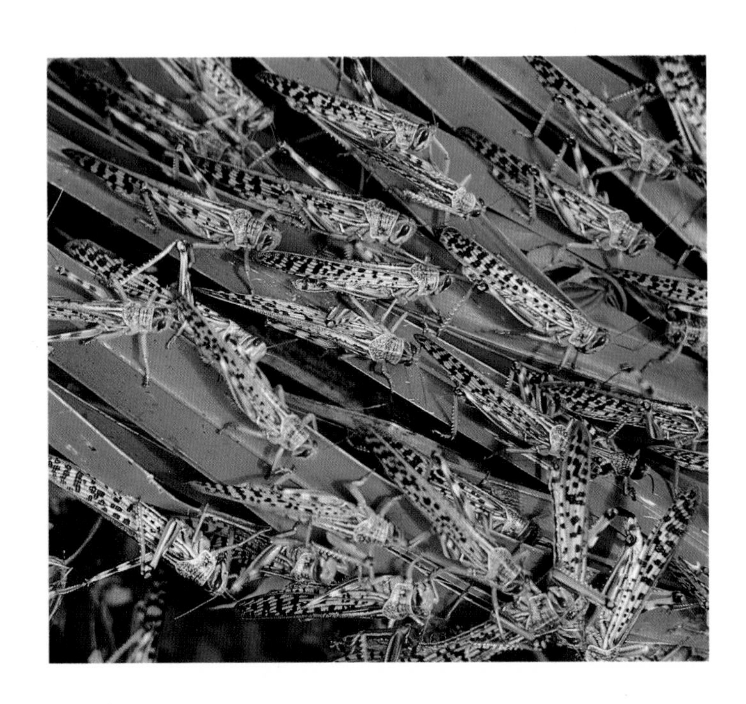

Scorpions are related to crabs and spiders. They have eight legs, claws for grabbing their prey and a curved tail tipped with a poisonous sting.

During the day the scorpion rests out of the sun in a burrow or under a stone. It hunts at dusk.

Baby scorpions cling to their mother's back when they first hatch. As they grow bigger their hard skin becomes too tight. Eventually it splits and a new skin forms underneath. The scorpion sheds its skin six or seven times before it is fully grown. After their first moult the babies leave their mother's back to look after themselves.

North America

Death Valley in the Great American Desert is the hottest place on earth. But it rains twice a year, so even here plants and animals survive.

Some plants make millions of tiny seeds that lie in the ground until it rains. Then they grow and flower quickly to make more seeds.

Cacti survive by storing water each time it rains. The water is stored in the fleshy leaves and the thick smooth skins stop the water evaporating in the heat. The giant saguaro cactus grows very slowly but after 100 years it can be 15 metres (50 feet) tall. The cactus' spines help protect it from animals who may try to tear open the leaves to get to the water.

Insects, kangaroo rats and other small animals feed on seeds and shoots. They come out at night when it is cool. The jackrabbit is a grazer, it eats grass and shoots. During the day it rests in the shade of a cactus or a stone.

The plant-eaters are hunted by the predators. Kangaroo rats and jackrabbits are hunted by bobcats, foxes and owls. Lizards eat the insects. The lizards in turn, are eaten by snakes and by birds like the roadrunner.

Kangaroo rats and bobcats

Kangaroo rats are very common in the American desert. Just before dusk they come out of their burrows, take a dust bath in the sand and start hunting for food.

The kangaroo rat stores seeds in pouches in its cheeks like a hamster to take back to its nest. If they are damp it buries them in the sand until they dry out.

The bobcat is much bigger than a pet cat. It is a fierce hunter. It usually hunts small animals like rats but sometimes it will attack an animal as large as a deer. Most of the bobcat's prey can run faster than it can, so it stalks silently and leaps from a tree or rock.

At the beginning of spring the female has 2 or 3 kittens. They are born in a cave or under a tree. At first they are blind but after ten days their eyes open. They feed on their mother's milk until the end of spring. They stay with her, learning to hunt, until the autumn.

The roadrunner and the poorwill

The roadrunner catches its prey on the ground. It runs after insects, lizards and small mammals. It is so quick it can even catch rattle-snakes. It darts about to keep out of the way of the snake's fangs and stabs it with its sharp beak.

The female roadrunner lays her eggs in a basket-shaped nest on the ground. When the chicks hatch they are helpless. The parents feed them on lizards – some are nearly as big as the chicks themselves.

The poorwill feeds on the wing. It flies at dusk, scooping up insects in its wide beak. In winter the poorwill finds a hole in the rocks and settles down to sleep for weeks on end. It breathes very slowly. This saves energy and water. Mammals like bears and dormice hibernate like this but very few birds do.

The poorwill nests on the ground. Its colours make it hard to see on the sand and rocks. If there is a predator nearby it can make a whistling sound exactly like a rattlesnake to frighten it away.

Snakes and lizards

The gopher snake is quite a long snake, up to 2.5m (8 ft) long. It is a good climber and can burrow well. It is usually active during the day, but if the weather is very hot it will become nocturnal and hunt at night. It feeds on lizards, rodents and birds. It kills its prey by constriction. This means it wraps its coils around the animal and squeezes until the prey is dead.

Rattlesnakes are deaf and cannot hear their own rattles. They rattle to warn large animals that they are nearby so that they do not get stepped on. The rattle is made from rings of hard skin at the tip of the snake's tail.

The sidewinder is a desert rattlesnake which moves across the sand by winding to and fro in big loops. It leaves very unusual tracks.

Most lizards are not poisonous but the gila monster is. Its bright skin signals danger. It feeds on small animals and eggs. When there is plenty of food it gets very fat. It can then go for months without eating.

Spadefoot toads and honeydew ants

Frogs and toads lay their eggs in water. You might think that they cannot live in the dry desert, but the spadefoot toad does. As soon as the rains come, the female lays her eggs in a pool. They hatch into tadpoles in just two or three days. The tadpoles grow into adults in less than five weeks.

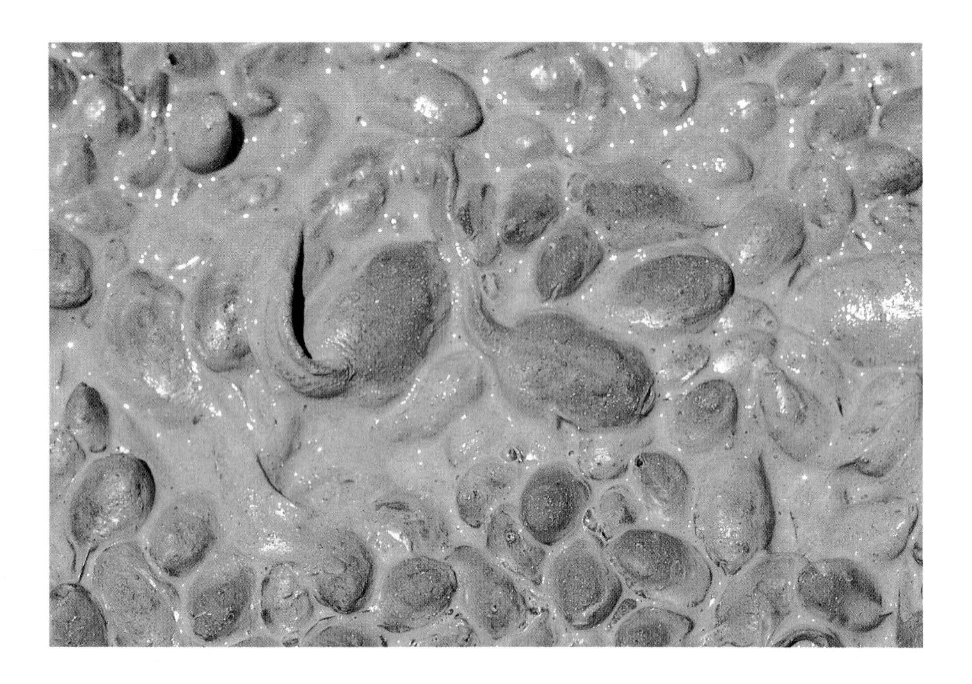

During the day the toad buries itself in the ground to keep cool. It digs itself in with its spade-shaped back feet. At night it comes out to catch spiders and insects with its long sticky tongue.

The entrance to the honeydew ants' nest is a small mound of sand a few inches high. Tunnels slant down from the entrance into the ground. At night, worker ants collect honeydew – a sugary liquid given out by insects that feed on plants. They bring it back to the nest and feed it to other ants who act as honey jars. These ants get so full they swell up like grapes. They hang from the ceiling until their food is needed.

Asia

The Gobi Desert in Asia is colder than Death Valley and the Sahara, especially in winter, but it is just as dry and harsh.

The bactrian camels in the Gobi Desert are the last wild camels in the world. They have two humps and grow thick winter coats to keep out the cold. There are less than 500 left in the wild.

Wild camels live in small family groups. The females have a baby every other year. The new baby has no humps. At first it finds it hard to stand on its long legs, but after a few hours it can run and follow the others. Its mother feeds it for two years and it stays with the family until it is four. After five years the camel is fully grown. Camels can live until they are fifty years old.

The wild ass was once common in deserts and grasslands all over Asia. But, now it is rare because it has been hunted for sport and food. Fortunately in some places it is protected and numbers are starting to increase again.

Gerbils, desert hedgehogs and Seveline's mouse

Gerbils are common in the deserts and grasslands of both Asia and Africa. They lead similar lives to jerboas and kangaroo rats, moving about quickly on their long back legs, collecting seeds.

Gerbils live in colonies. The females have 3–6 babies at a time in an underground nest lined with grass. The new babies are blind and helpless but they grow very fast. They are ready to start their own families after just three months.

Seveline's mouse, the desert dormouse and the desert hedgehog feed on insects, spiders and grubs. Seveline's mouse eats its own weight in insects every day. It lives in the cool deserts of Asia and has thick fur that grows very quickly.

The desert hedgehog is just like the hedgehogs that are common in gardens and woods in Europe. Hedgehogs are not found in America. If it is attacked the hedgehog rolls up into a tight ball with its spines sticking out. This makes it very difficult for a predator to bite it. The desert dormouse digs a burrow in which it hibernates during the winter.

Australia

The deserts in the middle of Australia are hot and dry. In some places they are rocky. In others there is sand or clay. At the edges the desert changes into dry grasslands.

The animals of Australia are very different from those in other places. Many of the furry animals are marsupials. These are mammals which have tiny babies that grow and feed in a pouch on their mother.

Some marsupials manage to live in the heat of the desert.

To save water the red kangaroo only sweats when it is hopping. When it stands still it licks its arms and shoulders to keep cool. During the hottest part of the day it crouches in the shade of a bush.

The rabbit-eared bandicoot does not sweat at all. It must stay underground to keep cool. It comes out at night to feed on insects and small lizards.

The marsupial mole is rarely seen in the wild. It spends its life burrowing through the sand eating grubs and larvae. Its tiny eyes are covered with fur so it cannot see.

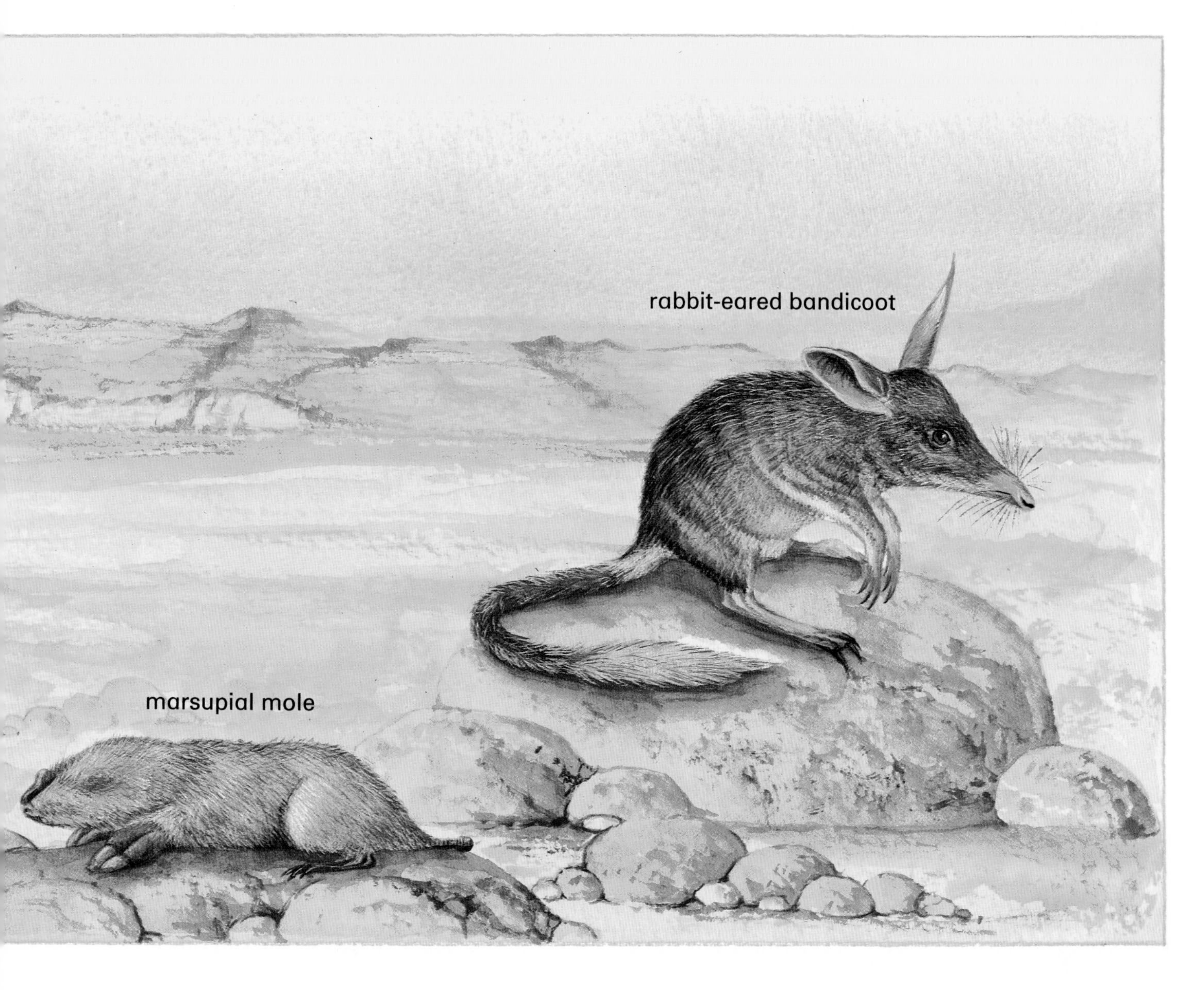

Lizards

Lizards are very common in Australia. There are more than 100 different kinds in the desert.

A lizard's skin is scaly. It must be waterproof to stop the lizard drying out in the sun, and tough to protect it from predators and rough stones.

Some skinks have smooth skins and short legs to help them swim through the sand, where it's cooler than above ground. The blue-tongued skink is sand-coloured to camouflage it from snakes and eagles. But when the male wants to attract a mate or frighten off a rival, he opens his mouth to show his bright blue tongue.

The bearded dragon's skin is usually orange but if it is threatened it suddenly turns black and faces sideways to show off its spikes.

The thorny devil is a small lizard just 15cm (6 inches) long. Its skin is covered in sharp spikes to protect it from predators.

Monitors are huge lizards. Some of them are 2.5m (8 ft) long. They hunt during the day. They are hunted by the Australian aborigines for food.